D0583341

Stonehenge

GREAT STRUCTURES IN HISTORY

Other titles in the Great Structures in History
series include:

The Great Wall of China
A Medieval Castle
The Panama Canal
The Roman Colosseum

Stonehenge

GREAT STRUCTURES IN HISTORY

Rachel Lynette

KIDHAVEN PRESS

An imprint of Thomson Gale, a part of The Thomson Corporation

THOMSON

™

GALE

Detroit • New York • San Francisco • San Diego • New Haven, Conn.
Waterville, Maine • London • Munich

© 2005 by Thomson Gale, a part of The Thomson Corporation.

Thomson, Star Logo and KidHaven Press are trademarks and Gale is a registered trademark used herein under license.

For more information, contact
KidHaven Press
27500 Drake Rd.
Farmington Hills, MI 48331-3535
Or you can visit our Internet site at http://www.gale.com

LIBRARY OF CONGRESS CATALOGING-IN-PUBLICATION DATA

Lynette, Rachel, 1964-
  Stonehenge / by Rachel Lynette.
      p. cm.--(Great structures in history)
  Includes bibliographical references.
Summary: Discusses Stonehenge, including why it was built, who built it, how it was constructed, how it was used, its deterioration, and its repair and restoration.
  ISBN 0-7377-1562-6
1. Stonehenge (United Kingdom)--History--Juvenile Literature. [Stonehenge (United Kingdom)--History.] I. Title. II. Series.

Printed in the United States of America

CONTENTS

CHAPTER ONE

Stonehenge Past and Present

Every year, thousands of people from all over the world come to England to visit Stonehenge. At first glance, Stonehenge appears to be an unorganized group of giant stones, some fallen and broken, others still standing upright. A few are in the shape of an upside-down U, with two upright stones holding a third stone on top of them. It is this last formation that gives Stonehenge its name. *Henge* means "hanging," so *Stonehenge* is translated as "hanging stones." Although Stonehenge has been damaged both by people and the weather, it still has a definite circular shape.

In many ways, Stonehenge is not unlike thousands of prehistoric stone rings scattered all across Great Britain. However, Stonehenge is different from these structures in several ways. Only Stonehenge was built with stones that had to be brought from many miles away. Stonehenge also contains some of the largest stones in the area. In addition, the design of Stonehenge is unique in all of England.

The Salisbury Plain

Stonehenge is located in the southern part of England in an area called the Salisbury Plain. Within this twelve-square-mile (nineteen-square-kilometer) space, only about half the size of Manhattan Island, stand the ruins of hundreds of other prehistoric monuments, many of them older than Stonehenge. In addition, the area around Stonehenge is dotted with hundreds of **barrows,** or burial pits. Some of these barrows are small, containing the remains of a single person, while others are communal graves for as many as forty.

The Original Stonehenge

No one knows exactly what Stonehenge looked like when it was completed. Although only forty stones remain today, **archaeologists** believe that about 162 stones made up the original structure. **Excavations** of the site have uncovered evidence of these missing stones and the patterns they formed. Ancient building tools, bits of stone, filled-in holes, and even human remains are important clues. These clues,

Druids gather at Stonehenge to celebrate the summer solstice.

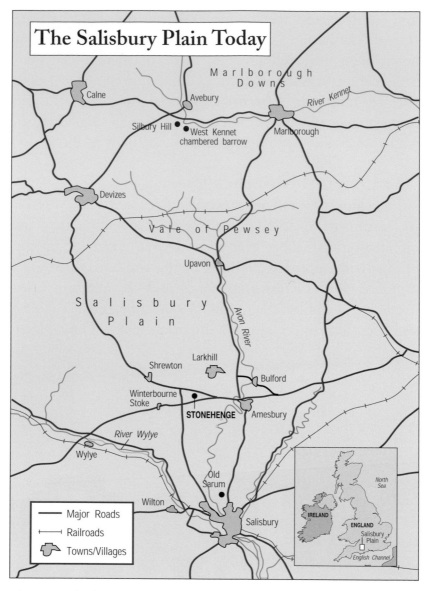

The Salisbury Plain Today

Marlborough Downs

Calne

Avebury

River Kennet

Silbury Hill
West Kennet
chambered barrow

Marlborough

Devizes

V a l e   o f   P e w s e y

Upavon

S a l i s b u r y
P l a i n

Avon River

Larkhill

Shrewton

Bulford

Winterbourne
Stoke

STONEHENGE   Amesbury

River Wylye

Wylye

Old
Sarum

Wilton

Salisbury

—— Major Roads
┼ Railroads
Towns/Villages

North
Sea

IRELAND

ENGLAND

Salisbury
Plain

English Channel

along with the stones that still remain, paint a picture of how Stonehenge may have looked thousands of years ago. Most archaeologists agree that the original structure included two outer rings of stones enclosing two horseshoe-shaped designs, with one long, flat stone in the center.

The first outer ring was constructed from a very hard type of sandstone called **sarsen**. Thirty of these stones were shaped into squared pillars and stood upright in a large circle. Each stone was just over 13 feet (4 meters) tall and about 7 feet (2.1 meters) wide. Horizontal stones, called **lintels**, were positioned atop the ring of standing stones to make a continuous circle. Most of the lintels and the smaller upright stones are gone. As with the rest of Stonehenge, no one knows what happened to them.

Within the sarsen circle was a second circle of about sixty smaller stones called bluestones. These shaped, blue gray stones were placed upright with no lintels. Most measured just under 7 feet (2.1 meters) and were about 4 feet (1.2 meters) wide. Only six of these stones are still standing. Others are on the ground, sometimes in pieces, and still others are missing altogether.

The bluestone circle surrounded a horseshoe of five giant sarsen **trilithons**. Each trilithon consisted of two large,

Today, only huge stones are left at Stonehenge, but archaeologists think that there were originally one hundred sixty-two.

upright stones that supported a single lintel, forming an upside-down U shape. Each trilithon stood alone. The lintels did not connect, as they did in the outer circle. The largest trilithon, positioned at the top of the horseshoe, was over 24 feet (7.3 meters) tall. Today, only one of the upright stones remains; the other two stones lie in pieces on the ground. Also in pieces is one of the smaller trilithons. However, three of these massive structures still stand.

Just within the trilithons stood a final horseshoe of nineteen upright bluestones. These shaped stones were 6 to 8 feet (1.8 to 2.4 meters) tall and about 2 feet (.61 meters) across. Only six of these stones still stand.

In the center of this inner horseshoe stood the Altar Stone. The Altar Stone was also made of sandstone, but a different type than the sarsens. It measured about 16 feet (4.9 meters) tall. This stone now lies on the ground, split in two.

The massive standing stones of Stonehenge are what most people come to see. However, Stonehenge also included other stones and earthworks, which were no doubt important to those who built it.

Earthworks of Stonehenge

Stonehenge is surrounded by a circle measuring 330 feet (100.5 meters) across. The circle was constructed only from the earth. At first, it consisted of a large ditch with a tall bank on the inside edge of the circle and a smaller bank on the outside edge, forming a double ring of raised earth. There is a break in the circle, called the Causeway, where it joins with a flat avenue about 35 feet (10.7 meters) wide. The avenue is bordered by earth banks and lines up directly with the open end of the stone horseshoes. Although it was probably quite dramatic when it was first formed, thousands of years of erosion have worn the circles down so that now the bottom of the ditch is only about 3 feet (.91 meters) below the top of the bank.

Fifty-six pits lie just within the earth circle. These pits, called Aubrey Holes after the scientist who discovered them, are not visible today. Archaeologists believe they were filled in soon after they were dug. Thirty-four of the pits have been excavated, and cremated human remains were found in most of them. There are also two round barrows placed directly across from each other.

Outlying Stones

The barrows were built around two of the original four Station Stones. These smaller sarsen blocks mark the corners of a perfect rectangle. Two of these stones still remain today.

The Slaughter Stone lies at the edge of the Causeway. This large sarsen stone is pitted with holes. At one time people thought it had been used for human sacrifices, and the purpose of the holes was to catch the blood of the victims.

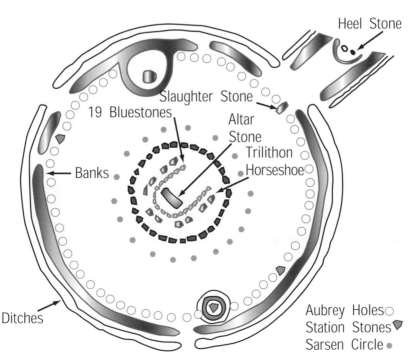

Stonehenge

These stones are all that is left of the Sarsen circle that was probably built more than four thousand years ago. It originally included thirty stones, each thirteen feet high and seven feet wide.

Scientists now believe that this stone was one of a pair, both originally standing upright, marking the entrance to the circle. They believe the holes were made later in an attempt to break the stone.

About 85 feet (26 meters) down the avenue stands the Heel Stone. This stone is untrimmed and measures 8 feet (2.4 meters) across and 16 feet (4.9 meters) high. Scientists believe this stone had a twin and that these two stones stood parallel to the Slaughter Stones. On the morning of the summer **solstice**, the sun would have risen directly between these two pairs of great stones.

Stonehenge was not built all at one time. Different parts of the structure were built by different groups of people, sometimes hundreds of years apart. There is evidence that some of the builders dismantled parts made by people before them in order to rebuild the monument in a different way. Although we do not know the complete history of Stonehenge, archaeologists and other scientists have used the clues left behind by these ancient peoples to form theories about how and when each part of Stonehenge came to be.

CHAPTER TWO

The Building of Stonehenge

Archaeologists believe that Stonehenge was constructed in three major phases over a period of about two thousand years. Archaeologists use a process called **radiocarbon dating** to discover the age of artifacts found at the site. By measuring the amount of carbon left in an artifact, scientists can determine how old it is. In this way, archaeologists have determined that the first two phases of Stonehenge were built about five thousand years ago, between 3100 and 2100 B.C.

The Early Phases

The first phase of Stonehenge included the circle of earth that surrounds the stones, the Aubrey Holes, the Heel Stone, and some wooden structures that have long since disappeared. The people who built the earliest phase lived in the Stone Age and had only primitive tools with which to work. Archaeologists have found shovels made from the shoulder blades of oxen and picks made from red deer antlers. It probably took several hundred workers to dig the circular ditch and build the double bank. Most archaeologists also believe that the four Station Stones were brought to Stonehenge toward the end of this period.

Nothing further was done at Stonehenge for hundreds of years; some archaeologists think the site might even have been abandoned. Then around 2500 B.C., a group of people called the Beakers began the second phase. Artifacts from this period indicate that these people were more advanced than those who began Stonehenge. They wore colorful woven clothes rather than animal hides, and they made pottery and used tools made of bronze. They also traded with other tribes.

Archaeologists excavated these ancient stone axes and arrowheads at Stonehenge.

The Beakers brought in the Altar Stone and several dozen bluestones from southwestern Wales. The four-ton stones were floated on the water or dragged across the land over 240 miles (386 kilometers) to the Stonehenge site. These stones were then placed in holes that were dug to form two half circles, one within the other. For reasons unknown, this design was never completed. Around 2100 B.C., the bluestones were removed and the holes filled in.

The Third Phase

The third phase of Stonehenge is the stone monument with which most people are familiar. The people who built this part of Stonehenge were from the Wessex culture. The project was probably overseen by a small group of powerful leaders who were wealthy enough to feed, house, and probably pay the thousands of laborers needed to complete the project. The bulk of the work—constructing the five large trilithons and the sarsen circle—was done in a period of less than one hundred years, from 2100 to 2000 B.C. The sarsen stones for this phase came from a quarry about twenty miles (thirty-two kilometers) away.

Moving the Stones

There are several theories about how these giant stones were moved. One possibility is that they were moved over land using logs as rollers. Using this method, the large stone would travel over a long line of logs placed one right after the other. After the stone passed over a log, the log would be carried to the front of the line. Scientists estimate that it took five hundred workers just to move one of the fifteen large sarsens over the logs. Another two hundred workers would have been needed to move the logs and clear the path. Using this method, it would have taken at least seven years to move the fifteen giant stones of the trilithons and many more years to move the smaller sarsens that formed the stone circle.

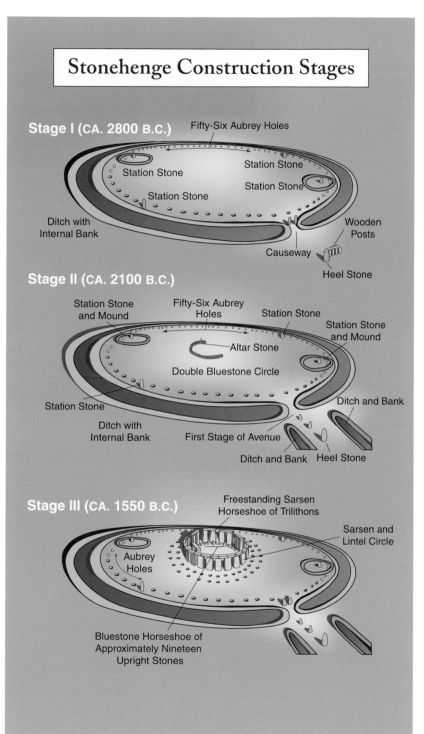

Stonehenge Construction Stages

Stage I (CA. 2800 B.C.)

Fifty-Six Aubrey Holes

Station Stone

Station Stone

Station Stone

Station Stone

Ditch with Internal Bank

Causeway

Wooden Posts

Heel Stone

Stage II (CA. 2100 B.C.)

Station Stone and Mound

Fifty-Six Aubrey Holes

Station Stone

Station Stone and Mound

Altar Stone

Double Bluestone Circle

Station Stone

Ditch with Internal Bank

First Stage of Avenue

Ditch and Bank

Ditch and Bank   Heel Stone

Stage III (CA. 1550 B.C.)

Freestanding Sarsen Horseshoe of Trilithons

Sarsen and Lintel Circle

Aubrey Holes

Bluestone Horseshoe of Approximately Nineteen Upright Stones

Workers use long lines of logs to roll the sarsen stones from the quarry to the building site.

Another possibility is that the stones were moved only during the winter when the ground was covered with ice and snow. Most of the land on the route from the quarry slopes gently downward. It would have only taken about twenty-five men to move each stone using this method.

The stones may have been moved as far as possible each winter and then left to sit through the rest of the year until they could be moved over the ice again.

A third possibility is that the Avon River was dammed to make it deeper and that the stones traveled most of the way down the river on large rafts. This would have left only a few miles for the stones to travel by rollers on the land. No matter how the stones were moved, we can be certain that it took many years and many workers to accomplish the task.

Shaping the Stones

Once the stones reached the site, they had to be carved into the right size and shape. The bottom was shaped into

The mortise joints carefully carved into both ends of this lintel stone were fitted into the tenon joints of the upright stones, making the structure stable.

a dull point, like a giant stake. The sides were made rectangular and smooth. Some of the stones were polished, while others were left rough. Sarsen is a very hard type of sandstone, and the people doing the work had only primitive tools. Archaeologists estimate it would have taken over five hundred thousand hours of hard labor just to shape the stones.

The builders also carved the stones to fit together. The upright stones were carved with a bump at the top called a **tenon joint**. The lintels had hollow, bowl-shaped spaces called **mortise joints** carved on their undersides. The mortise joints fit onto the tenon joints, thus making the structure more stable.

Placing the Stones

After the stones were shaped, they had to be put into the correct positions. Each upright stone was leveraged into a hole. The holes were dug according to the size of the stones. Larger stones needed larger holes. The largest sarsen required a hole 8 feet (2.4 meters) deep. Archaeologists believe that a system of ropes and pulleys was used to pull the stones upright. It probably took about two hundred men to pull each of the larger stones into place. Once a stone was standing straight, the hole was filled in with dirt and packed down. The stones were then left to settle for several months before further work could be done.

The final and perhaps the biggest challenge was how to place the giant lintels on top of the upright stones. Most archaeologists think that the lintels were lifted using a tower of logs. The stone was first leveraged onto a platform of logs, which was carefully positioned next to the upright stones. Then one end of the stone was raised, and another layer of logs was placed under it. The same thing was done under the other end. This raised the stone the height of one layer of logs, probably between one and two

These workers are using a lever to raise the giant stone. Other workers put more logs under each end of the stone. Eventually, it can be leveraged into place on top of the upright stones.

feet (thirty and sixty centimeters). In this way, the lintel was slowly raised until it could be levered into place.

More work was done on Stonehenge between 2000 and 1100 B.C. The remaining outlying stones were brought in and placed. The bluestones from the second phase were brought back to the site and used to form the circle of standing stones just within the sarsen circle and the horseshoe just within the horseshoe of trilithons. Another series of holes was dug in a double circle around the stone monument. These holes, called the X and Y holes, were probably meant to hold another set of stones. For reasons unknown, this part of the project was

Today only three complete trilithons still stand. Originally, a horseshoe of five massive trilithons and several smaller ones stood inside the bluestone circle.

never completed. No additional stones were brought to Stonehenge, and the holes were eventually filled in.

Thousands of people spanning many generations worked to build Stonehenge. It required more labor and wealth to build Stonehenge than any other prehistoric monument in Great Britain. Archaeologists have unearthed many clues to help them discover how Stonehenge was constructed. Discovering why it was built and what it was used for is an even more challenging task.

CHAPTER THREE

The Mystery of Stonehenge

For thousands of years, people have wondered why Stonehenge was built. People have imagined that the structure was for used for all kinds of things, including an ancient sports stadium, a burial ground, and even as a signal for UFOs to land. Ideas about Stonehenge's purpose have changed throughout the ages. Early theories tended to feature some sort of magic. This is probably because people in the Middle Ages could not imagine how the giant stones could have been moved and erected without the use of magic.

Early Theories

One of the first stories about how Stonehenge was constructed and what it was used for was written in the twelfth century by Geoffrey of Monmouth. In his book, *History of the Kings of Britain,* Geoffrey claims that the wizard Merlin built Stonehenge for King Ambrosius in A.D. 485. Ambrosius wanted the structure built as a monument to the soldiers who had fallen in a battle against the Saxons. According to Geoffrey, Merlin used magic and machines to transport the stones and to build Stonehenge. Although it was a popular and often widely believed story, we now know that Stonehenge was constructed nearly two thousand years before Ambrosius ruled Britain.

In the seventeenth century, John Aubrey wrote that Stonehenge was built and used by the **Druids**. The Druids were Celtic priests who lived in Britain around 250 B.C. Aubrey and others believed that the Druids used magic to build Stonehenge and then used the site for **pagan** rituals and celebrations. Some even believe that the

This aerial view of Stonehenge shows that the original structure had a long, flat stone in the center surrounded by two horseshoe-shaped designs. Two rings made up of huge stones circled the whole area.

Druids held human sacrifices at Stonehenge. Modern Druids denounce the idea of human sacrifices, but they do claim a connection with Stonehenge. They believe that most of the evidence that Druids once used the site was stolen or destroyed during excavations. Archaeologists know that the Druids did not construct Stonehenge, but there is no way to know for sure that they did not use the site for their ceremonies.

Recent theories focus on the placement of the stones and how they relate to certain astronomical events. Scientists who study the beliefs and customs of ancient

Thousands of people came to Stonehenge every year to take part in pagan rituals and attend the elaborate ceremonies and celebrations on the winter and summer solstices.

cultures about the heavens are called **archaeoastronomers**. Archaeoastronomers have made important and interesting discoveries at Stonehenge.

Stonehenge and the Sun

William Stukeley was the first scientist to connect Stonehenge with astronomy. In 1740 he realized that Stonehenge could be used to predict the summer solstice. On the summer solstice, which is the longest day of the year, the sun rises directly over the Heel Stone. This means the sunrise lines up with the Causeway and the open parts of the stone horseshoes.

We know that the summer solstice occurs around June 21 each year. But ancient people did not have calendars. They judged the time of year by the seasons. Knowing the time of year was very important for crop planting. If farmers planted their crops too early, the young plants could be destroyed by a spring frost. If they planted too late, the harvest could be ruined by an early frost. By identifying a single day in the year, people could count forward to figure out the best time to plant. Knowing when the summer solstice would occur might also have helped priests and leaders.

Seeing the sun rise directly over the Heel Stone inspires awe even today. This event must have caused similar feelings in ancient peoples. A person who could predict this wondrous event would have been highly respected, perhaps even feared. It may be that the priests of Stonehenge were very powerful. These priests probably held elaborate ceremonies on the solstices, which served to further awe the common people.

Stonehenge and the Moon

In the early 1960s, the English astronomer Gerald Hawkins used technology to formulate new theories about how

Over the years, scientists have been surprised to find that many of the upright stones are related to the night sky or to astrological events.

ancient people may have used Stonehenge. Hawkins was especially interested in how the stones lined up with each other and how those alignments related to the night sky. Hawkins knew that it would take a great deal of work to do all of the math needed to show the different ways that the stones lined up. Instead of doing all this work himself, he used an IBM computer. The results surprised even him.

Hawkins found Stukeley's summer and winter solstice alignments as well as other alignments related to the sun. In addition, he found that many of the stones were aligned to show the rising and setting of the moon at different times of the year. But his most controversial theory was focused on the Aubrey Holes.

Predicting Lunar Eclipses

Hawkins found that if a person put markers in certain holes and moved them to adjacent holes at the right time each year, he would be able to predict when a **lunar eclipse** would occur. Lunar eclipses occur every 18.6 years. Multiplying this number by three and rounding off gives a result of fifty-six; the exact number of the Aubrey Holes. It may be that the ancient priests who ruled Stonehenge used their ability to predict lunar eclipses to increase their own power. By knowing when an eclipse would occur, they could have made it seem like they were causing the sky to turn dark. Hawkins believed the holes were dug for just this reason.

Hawkins wrote a book called *Stonehenge Revealed*. Although the book was widely read and praised by many people, there were also many critics. Hawkins's biggest critic was archaeologist Richard Atkinson. Atkinson spent a lifetime studying Stonehenge and felt that Hawkins's ideas were based on inaccurate measurements and poor logic. He especially opposed the eclipse theory, pointing out that the Aubrey Holes were filled in soon after they were dug.

We may never know what Stonehenge was used for or why it was built. It was probably used for many different things over the years. It was most certainly considered to be a sacred place. Ceremonies were probably held there. We know from the human remains found at the site that it was also used as a burial site. Many people have speculated that at least some of the people buried at Stonehenge were victims of human sacrifices, but there is no way to know how these people died. Most archaeologists agree that Stonehenge does have some connection to celestial events. At the very least, Stonehenge was probably used to predict and celebrate the summer solstice.

Some of the stones can be used to predict when a lunar eclipse will occur. Ancient priests may have used this knowledge to increase their power over the people.

These skeletons found in burial sites at Stonehenge may have been victims of human sacrifice.

To some extent, the history of Stonehenge will always be a mystery, but the future of Stonehenge is within our control. If future generations are to enjoy the monument, efforts must be made today to preserve it.

CHAPTER FOUR

Stonehenge Today and Tomorrow

A lthough still awe inspiring, Stonehenge is a mere shadow of what it once was. Most of the original stones are missing, and the ones that remain have suffered severe damage. The weather has caused some of the damage. Centuries of rain, snow, and wind have worn away at the stones and their foundations. Sadly, most of the damage was done not by the elements, but by people.

People and Stonehenge

When Stonehenge was built, the priests and leaders who ruled it protected it from damage. It was most likely thought of as a sacred place that no one would dare to harm in any way. However, things changed in the first few hundred years A.D. Christianity was spreading throughout Europe. Many early Christians believed that the older pagan religions were evil, and they damaged many places sacred to non-Christians, including Stonehenge. Stones were toppled and shattered intentionally. Between the eleventh and fourteenth centuries, medieval peasants raided Stonehenge. Large chunks of stone were hauled away and used to build houses and other structures.

From the 1700s through most of the 1900s the fate of Stonehenge was in the hands of whoever happened to own the property at the time. Some left the site open for visitors, some did not. In 1898 the owner built a fence around the monument and charged admission. Early tourists were not always kind to the monument. Many carved off small pieces because they believed that they held magical powers. They believed that when ground to a powder and made into a tea, the stones could cure illness. People also took pieces of the monument for souvenirs or carved their names into the stones. Other people brought ladders and climbed to the top of the stones, damaging them further.

This protest against the British government is just one of the many events such as music festivals and military training that have caused severe damage to the once-sacred place.

In 1958 a crane was used to lift one of the eighteen-ton lintels of a fallen trilithon back into place as part of a restoration project.

Stonehenge in the Twentieth Century

In 1901 architect William Gowland began a restoration project. Under his supervision, workers straightened several dangerously leaning stones and strengthened their foundations with concrete. More restoration was completed between 1919 and 1964. Fallen lintels were lifted back onto their original upright stones, and more concrete was added to the foundations.

In 1915 Stonehenge was owned by Cecil Chubb, who had bought the monument and the land surrounding it at an auction. Three years later, in 1918, Chubb donated the site to the English government. Although it was owned by the government, it still was not protected from harm. From 1919 to 1926, amateur archaeologist Colonel William Hawley did significant damage to the site with his reckless excavating techniques.

Throughout the twentieth century, people continued to abuse Stonehenge and the surrounding area. In the 1970s and 1980s, the area was used for large summer music festivals. These festivals drew thousands of people who camped on the land for several days, leaving garbage and graffiti behind them. The military has used the area for training and weapons testing, destroying many nearby monuments. In addition, two major roads were built close to the stones, one of them running just a few feet from the Heel Stone. Many people feel that the pollution and vibrations from the traffic are further damaging the site.

Stonehenge Today

In 1986 Stonehenge became an official World Heritage Site. This means that like the great pyramids in Egypt and the Taj Mahal in India, Stonehenge is considered one of the world's most important places. Although Stonehenge belongs to the whole world, the English

Heritage Foundation is responsible for managing the site and protecting the monument.

Over eight hundred thousand people visit Stonehenge every year—as many as two thousand an hour during the busiest times. Visitors pay a small admission fee to wander on a guided path through the stones. A recorded audio tour is also available. Ropes keep people on the paths and protect the stones from damage. Visitors are no longer allowed to touch the stones. The site includes a visitor's center, refreshment stands, and a gift shop. Many people feel that Stonehenge is no longer the sacred place it once was. Visitors are often dismayed to find a crowded, noisy tourist trap rather than a special and sacred monument. The English Heritage Foundation has been working with several other organizations to improve the visitor's experience at Stonehenge while still protecting the monument.

The Future of Stonehenge

Renovating the Stonehenge site is a difficult task. Many people and organizations have opinions about how the monument should be preserved and what sort of access tourists should be given. The two major roads running through the site present additional challenges. Organizations concerned with the future of Stonehenge have come together to form the Stonehenge Project. The Stonehenge Project will take several years to complete, but most of it should be finished by 2008. The Stonehenge Project has three major goals for the site.

The first goal is to replace the visitor's center, which is small and located too close to the stones. The old center will be torn down, and a new visitor's center will be built 2 miles (3.2 kilometers) away. There will be a transit system to take visitors to the stones. The new center will include multimedia presentations, exhibition galleries, a gift shop, and a café. Visitors will be able to learn about the history of Stonehenge before they visit the monument.

The second goal focuses on the two major roads that run close to the stones. One of the roads will be closed. The other road will be rerouted underground. A 1.5-mile-long (2.4 kilometers) tunnel will be constructed for the part of the road that runs near the stones. This will make the site more attractive and peaceful.

The third goal is to restore the landscape around the monument. With the roads, visitor's center, and surrounding fences gone, the land will be returned to the grassy plain it once was. Visitors will be able to see Stonehenge in

These are some of the eight hundred thousand tourists who visit Stonehenge each year.

Pollution and vibrations from two major roads which were built just feet from Stonehenge are damaging the site.

a more natural setting and experience the monument as a special and sacred place.

Stonehenge will always be a place of mystery and awe. Although there are many clues about how it was built, the people who built it, and even what it was used for, there are still many unanswered questions. Perhaps, more than the stones themselves, it is this mystery that fascinates people and continues to draw them to this sacred place.

Glossary

archaeoastronomer: Someone who studies the astronomical beliefs, practices, and discoveries of ancient cultures.

archaeologist: Someone who studies the buildings, graves, tools, and other objects of people who lived in the past.

barrow: A large mound of earth placed over a burial site.

Druid: A priest in an ancient religion practiced in Britain, Ireland, and Gaul until the people of those areas were converted to Christianity.

excavation: The process of removing earth that covers very old objects buried in the ground in order to discover things about the past.

lintel: A horizontal beam joining two sides to form a doorway.

lunar eclipse: An eclipse of the moon caused by the earth passing between the sun and the moon and casting its shadow on the moon.

mortise joint: A hole formed to fit onto a bump in order to secure a joint.

pagan: Belonging to a religion that worships many gods, especially one that existed before the main world religions.

radiocarbon dating: A method for determining the age of an object by measuring the amount of carbon 14 remaining in the substance.

sarsen: Large sandstone blocks found in England.

solstice: Either of the times when the sun is farthest from the equator. The summer solstice occurs on or about June 21, and the winter solstice occurs on or about December 21.

tenon joint: A bump formed to fit into a hole in order to secure a joint.

trilithon: A prehistoric structure consisting of two large stones set upright to support a third on their tops.

For Further Reading

Books

Harriette Abels, *Stonehenge.* Mankato, MN: Crestwood House, 1987. This book tells the story of Stonehenge and includes a map of the area as well as a glossary.

Christopher Chippendale, *Stonehenge Complete.* New York: Thames and Hudson, 1994. This book gives a great deal of detail about Stonehenge and the people who built and studied it. There are 266 illustrations, including maps and diagrams, as well as many pictures of the monument.

Wendy Mass, *Stonehenge.* San Diego, CA: Lucent Books, 1998. This book gives details about the history of Stonehenge, focusing on the phases of construction, as well as restoration efforts. There is also a time line of important events.

Peter Roop and Connie Roop, *Stonehenge.* San Diego, CA: Greenhaven Press, 1989. This book covers a wide variety of theories about how and why Stonehenge was built. It also includes many interesting quotes from noted archaeologists who have studied the monument.

David Souden, *Stonehenge Revealed.* New York: Collins & Brown, 1997. This impressive book features detailed text and excellent pictures. There are color photos of Stonehenge as well as drawings, maps, and diagrams.

Web Sites

About Stonehenge.Info (www.aboutstonehenge.info). This site offers a wealth of information about Stonehenge, including a section on how to build "your own Stonehenge."

English Heritage (www.english-heritage.org). This site links to information about the history and future of Stonehenge.

Stonehenge (www.megalithia.com). This site offers information about Stonehenge as well as some excellent photos. Especially interesting is the animation on the history page, which shows the phases of construction.

Index

Picture Credits

Cover image: Corel
© Adam Woolfitt/CORBIS, 7
AP/Wide World Photos, 38
© Archivo Iconografico, S.A./CORBIS, 22
Chris Jouan, 18, 21
© English Heritage/Topham-HIP/The Image Works, 12, 19
© Gary Trotter; Eye Ubiquitous/CORBIS, 32–33
HIP/Scala/Art Resource, NY, 26
© Hulton/Archive by Getty Images, 34
© Kevin Schafer/CORBIS, 28
Madfred Gottschalk/Lonely Planet Images, 36–37
National Trust/Art Resource, NY, 25
© Philip Gould/CORBIS, 9
Photodisk, 28
© Richard T. Nowitz/CORBIS, 15, 31
© Roger Ressmeyer/CORBIS, 30

About the Author

Rachel Lynette has written four other books for KidHaven Press, as well as dozens of articles on children and family life. She has taught children of all ages and is currently working as a technology teacher in Seattle, Washington. Lynette lives in the Songaia Cohousing Community with her husband, Scott; her two children, David and Lucy; a cat named Cookie; and two playful rats. When she is not teaching or writing, she enjoys spending time with her family and friends, reading, drawing, biking, and rollerblading.